Dedicated to Gloria

ELEPHANT

They say an elephant never forgets...
And I know it's true as true can be.
That's because there's...
An elephant living inside of me!

Daddy says, "I told you to go outside and play."
"You did," I say because it's true.
"Then why didn't you do it?" he asks.
I say, "Because I was busy paddling a canoe."

Daddy shakes his head, then he smiles.
"Can you show me?" he says.
I give him a jacket; I hold him back...
"Pardon the elephant!" I say.

Daddy grabs a paddle and takes his end.
I have my paddle and sit at the other.
We are soon swish swishing out to sea.
"I hope you're wearing life jackets!" calls mother.

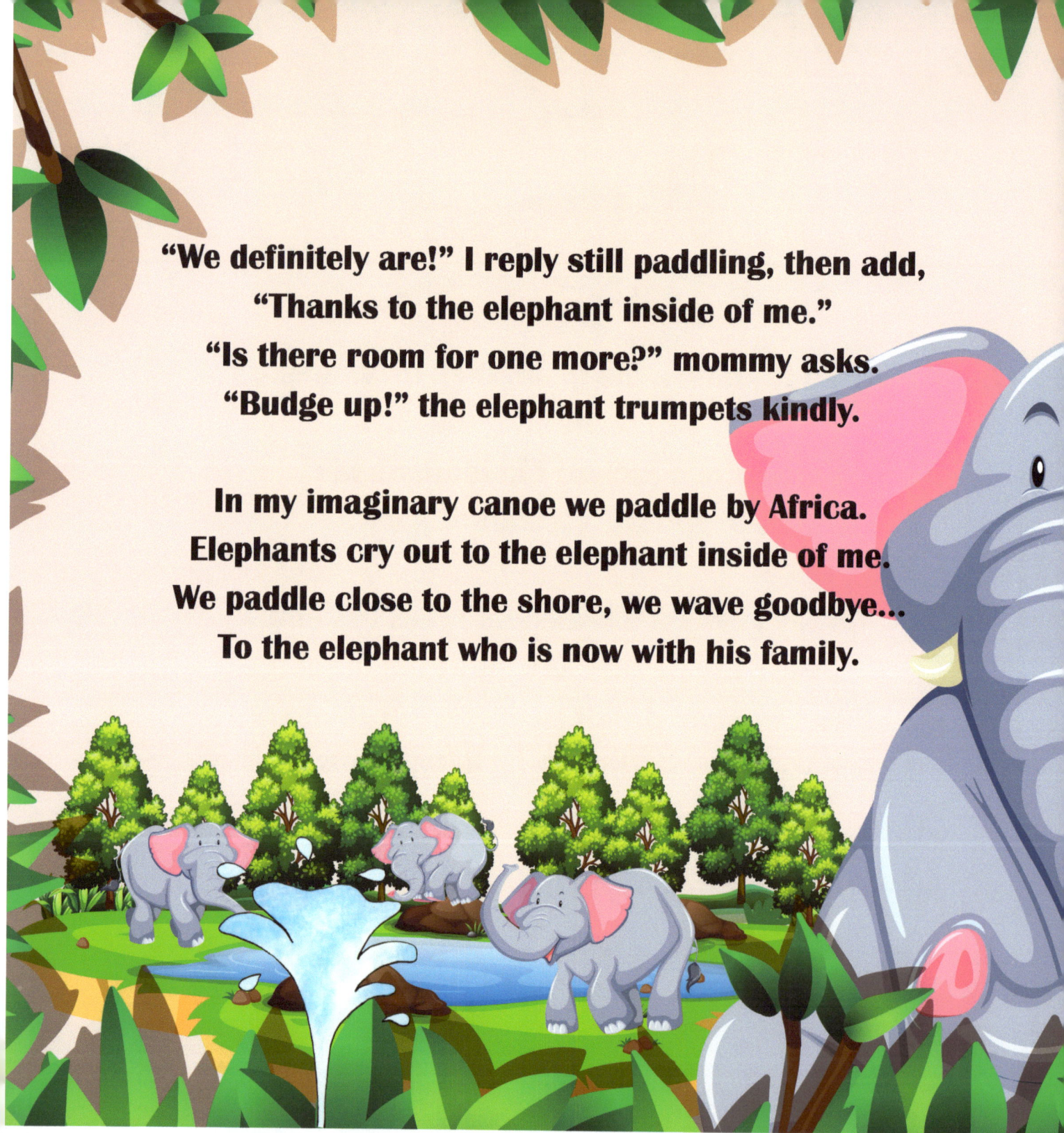

"We definitely are!" I reply still paddling, then add,
"Thanks to the elephant inside of me."
"Is there room for one more?" mommy asks.
"Budge up!" the elephant trumpets kindly.

In my imaginary canoe we paddle by Africa.
Elephants cry out to the elephant inside of me.
We paddle close to the shore, we wave goodbye...
To the elephant who is now with his family.

MOUSE

"When I'm sleeping over at my cousin's house...
There's a mouse inside of me.
I don't understand a single word he says.
All he does is "SQUEAK! SQUEAK! SQUEAK!" at me!

My tummy growls, so maybe he is hungry too?
Everyone's asleep so we go downstairs.
I'm not sure what mice like to eat.
I open the refrigerator doors and stare."

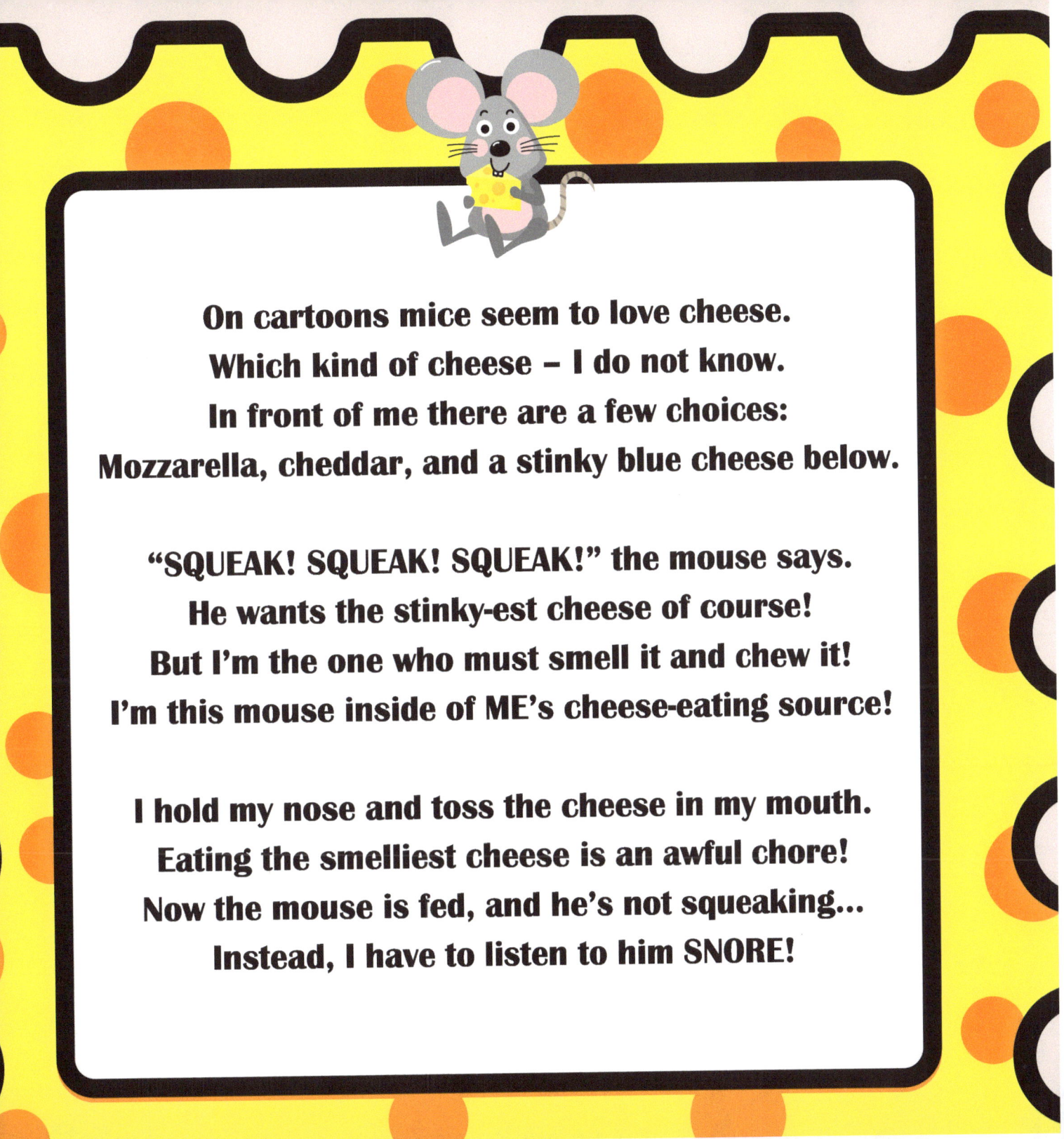

On cartoons mice seem to love cheese.
Which kind of cheese – I do not know.
In front of me there are a few choices:
Mozzarella, cheddar, and a stinky blue cheese below.

"SQUEAK! SQUEAK! SQUEAK!" the mouse says.
He wants the stinky-est cheese of course!
But I'm the one who must smell it and chew it!
I'm this mouse inside of ME's cheese-eating source!

I hold my nose and toss the cheese in my mouth.
Eating the smelliest cheese is an awful chore!
Now the mouse is fed, and he's not squeaking...
Instead, I have to listen to him SNORE!

When I sleep over at Grandma's house...
There's a wolf inside of me.
He wakes me up and says, "What big eyes you have!"
Then he laughs. He thinks he is so funny!

"Go to sleep!" I say. "Please go to sleep!"
He says, "That's not what you are meant to say!"
Unless I play along with the story line...
He refuses to go to sleep – or away!

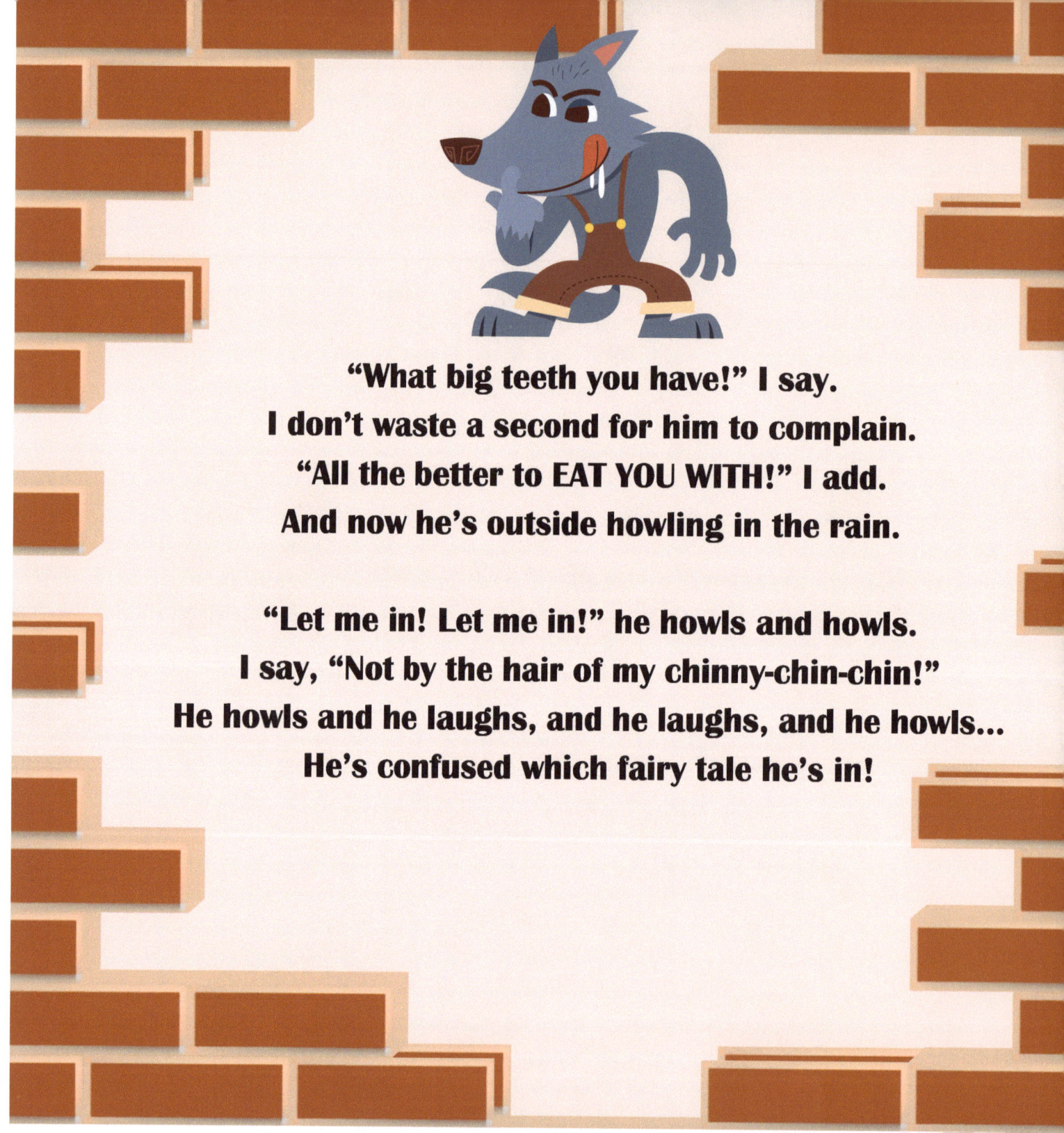

"What big teeth you have!" I say.
I don't waste a second for him to complain.
"All the better to EAT YOU WITH!" I add.
And now he's outside howling in the rain.

"Let me in! Let me in!" he howls and howls.
I say, "Not by the hair of my chinny-chin-chin!"
He howls and he laughs, and he laughs, and he howls...
He's confused which fairy tale he's in!

FIREFLY

"Come and dance with me fireflies!" I say.
They don't answer. They continue to glow.
Fireflies rave and flicker on and off.
When I'll see them again, I don't know.

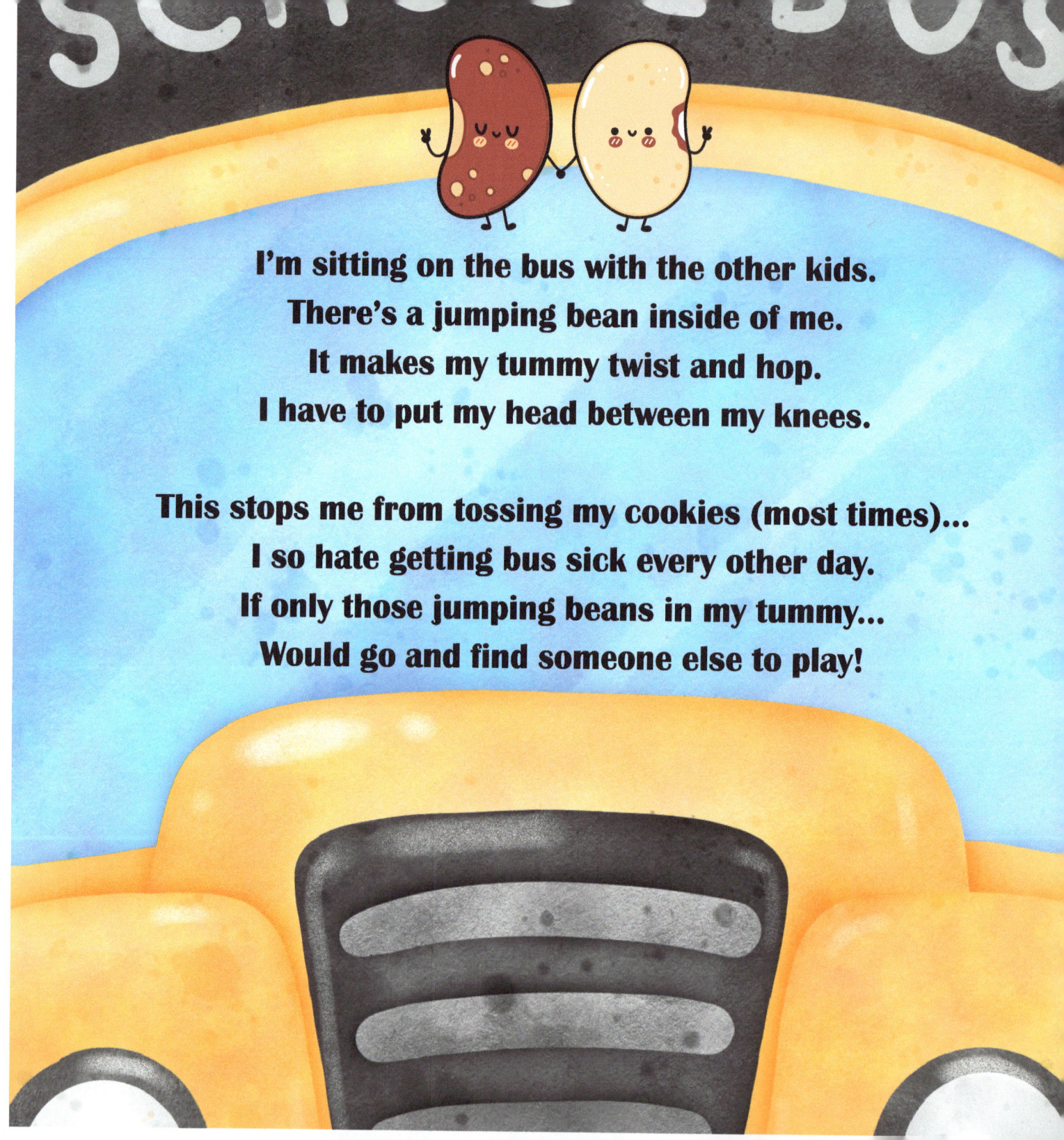

I'm sitting on the bus with the other kids.
There's a jumping bean inside of me.
It makes my tummy twist and hop.
I have to put my head between my knees.

This stops me from tossing my cookies (most times)...
I so hate getting bus sick every other day.
If only those jumping beans in my tummy...
Would go and find someone else to play!

POLAR BEAR

I dream of catching fish in the rivers and lakes.
Because there is a polar bear inside of me.
He visits not often, every now and then.
He visits me seasonally.

In the springtime he craves salmon.
We stand in the water waiting, side by side...
The school of salmon come in, jumping high.
We catch them – he eats them – with pride.

In the winter when there is snow everywhere
The polar bear can get lost in the blanket of white.
It's easier to find him later on...
Under the dark skies at night.

The polar bear inside of me and I are friends.
We tend to look after each other.
It's funny the way things turn out.
Because I always wanted a big brother!

JITTERBUG

Mom says, "Please stop that jitterbugging!"
I say, "I can't the jitterbug is inside of me!"
"Try to stop it, all the same," she suggests.
Still, I can't stop jiggling my knee!

And it's not just my knee that jiggles!
Sometimes it's every single bit of me.
And no matter how hard I try to stop it.
The jitterbug keeps jittering me!

TASMANIAN DEVIL

My bedroom is always a great big mess!
Because a Tasmanian Devil lives inside of me.
No matter how often I clean and dust.
That whirling menace makes it more messy!

"How CAN you LIVE LIKE THAT?!" my older
sister asks.
"Who asked for your opinion?" I say.
It's how to get rid of annoying unwanted questions.
Advice you might want to remember these days.

But I sure wish things could be different.
If this Tasmanian Devil would go.
Then I might be able to find my missing stuff...
Like my homework, my glasses and my pillow!

LOBSTER

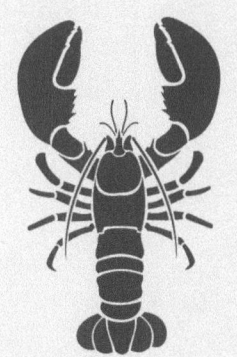

When I feel scared, I count to ten.
There's a decapod living inside of me.
You might know him better as a lobster.
He has ten legs you see!

Using his claws, he clicks as I count.
Yes, we're a lobster and me symphony!
When I get to 10, I'm no longer afraid.
Thanks to the lobster inside of me!

POPCORN

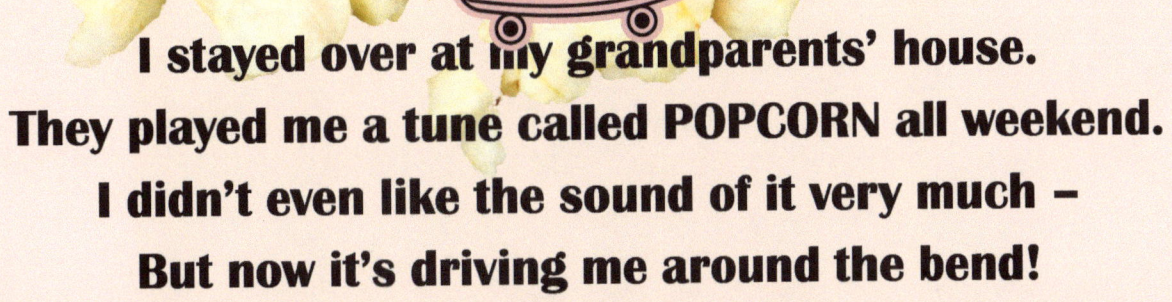

I stayed over at my grandparents' house.
They played me a tune called POPCORN all weekend.
I didn't even like the sound of it very much –
But now it's driving me around the bend!

All day and all-night POPCORN is popping in my head!
I can even taste the salt and smell the butter!
I go everywhere making POP! POP! POPPING sounds.
At school they look at me like I'm a nutter!

POP! POP! POP! Pop pop pop pop! On repeat.
But do you want to know something strange?
I'm not craving popcorn anymore!
I prefer fruit and veggies for a change!

DREAM

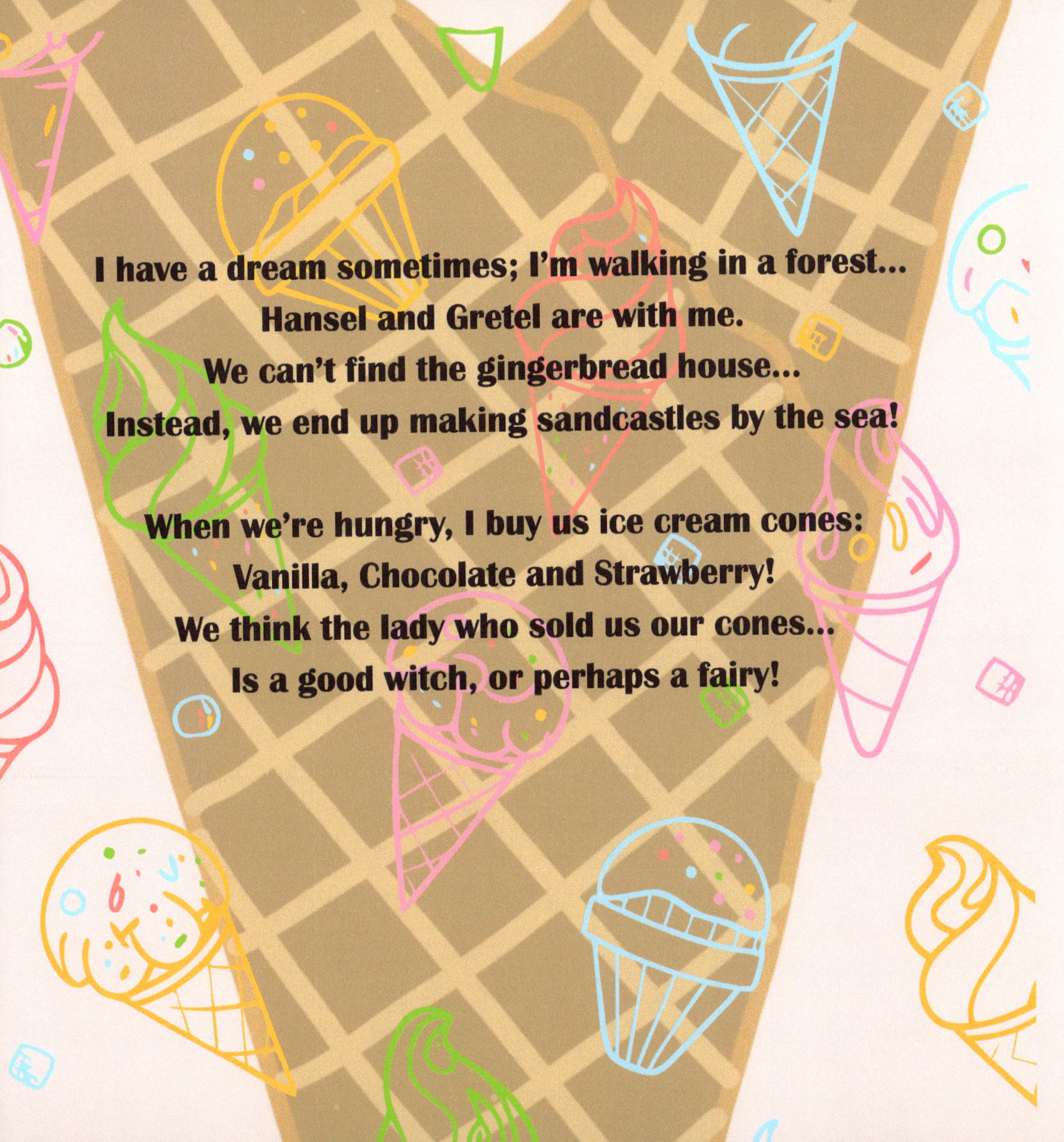

I have a dream sometimes; I'm walking in a forest...
Hansel and Gretel are with me.
We can't find the gingerbread house...
Instead, we end up making sandcastles by the sea!

When we're hungry, I buy us ice cream cones:
Vanilla, Chocolate and Strawberry!
We think the lady who sold us our cones...
Is a good witch, or perhaps a fairy!

OCTOPUS

Can you imagine what it's like...
Living with an octopus inside of me?
In total we have FOUR HEARTS!
Please don't say YOU'RE KIDDING ME!

It is difficult to sleep, and to be awake.
It's like I'm walking in fields of spaghetti.
My feet sink down, my spirits too.
Even though he is only imaginary!

Between us we have TEN ARMS...
Twelve if you include my knobby knees!
Makes me wonder with so many arms.
Who'll grab the tissue when I sneeze!

CHICKEN

There are some days –
When a chicken is inside of me.
He thinks the sky is falling...
And no matter what I say
he doesn't believe me.

"Come on outside, you'll see!" I say.
He hides his head, and he clucks.
"Everything will be okay," I say.
He shakes, shudders,
then adds more clucks.

I pick up the chicken and carry him in my arms.
First to the window, then to the door.
Outside, I lie on my back. He sits on my tummy...
We watch the floating clouds until they pour.

"I told you the sky is falling!" he explains.
I say, "It isn't. It's just the rain."
He opens his beak, drinks a few raindrops.
Then asks, "Next time the sky falls, would you please
bring me outside again?"

SPIDER

We went on holiday in the month of May.
I hoped for some family time for me.
I would be far, far away.
From the spider inside of me.

She spun herself a fine new web.
She caught flies and chose to stay behind.
With a clear head and heart...
I left her home, and she didn't mind.

"It's only for a few days," mommy and daddy say.
"We'll have so much fun, you'll see!"
"You'll hardly even miss her!"
I'm more worried she will be missing me!

UNICORN

I wait at the top of a very tall bridge.
For the unicorn who lives inside of me.
He comes and goes like the seasons.
Because my unicorn is free.

I see him far away on the horizon.
From the size of a dot, he grows.
As he comes nearer and nearer
I can see he is being followed by rainbows.

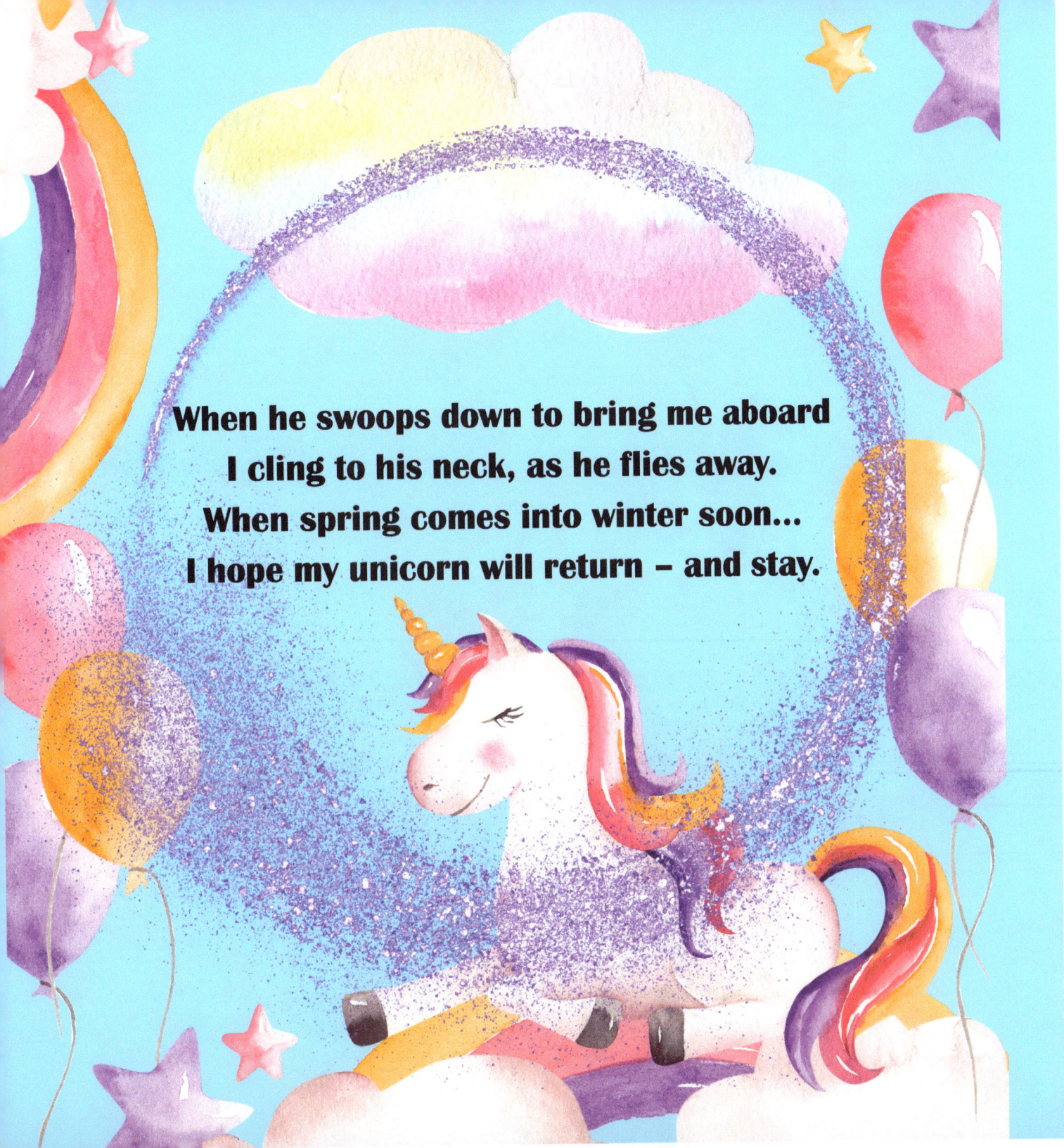

When he swoops down to bring me aboard
I cling to his neck, as he flies away.
When spring comes into winter soon...
I hope my unicorn will return – and stay.

FRIENDSHIP

Best friend

"Sometimes when you make a new friend.
Things between you seem to click into place.
Like you've known each other for a very long time.
Like you've shared another time and space.

But no matter how many new friends you make.
No friendships will ever compare.
To the ones surviving over the years...
Friendships like that are rare!

PUFFERFISH

When I'm out and about somewhere...
And a bully sets their sights on me.
I take defense and puff myself up.
Because there's a pufferfish inside of me.

I breathe in and out, deeply, rapidly.
I let the air fill me up with powerful energy.
PUFF! PUFF! PUFF! I grow and I grow!
So much so, that the bully runs away from me!

HOMING PIGEON

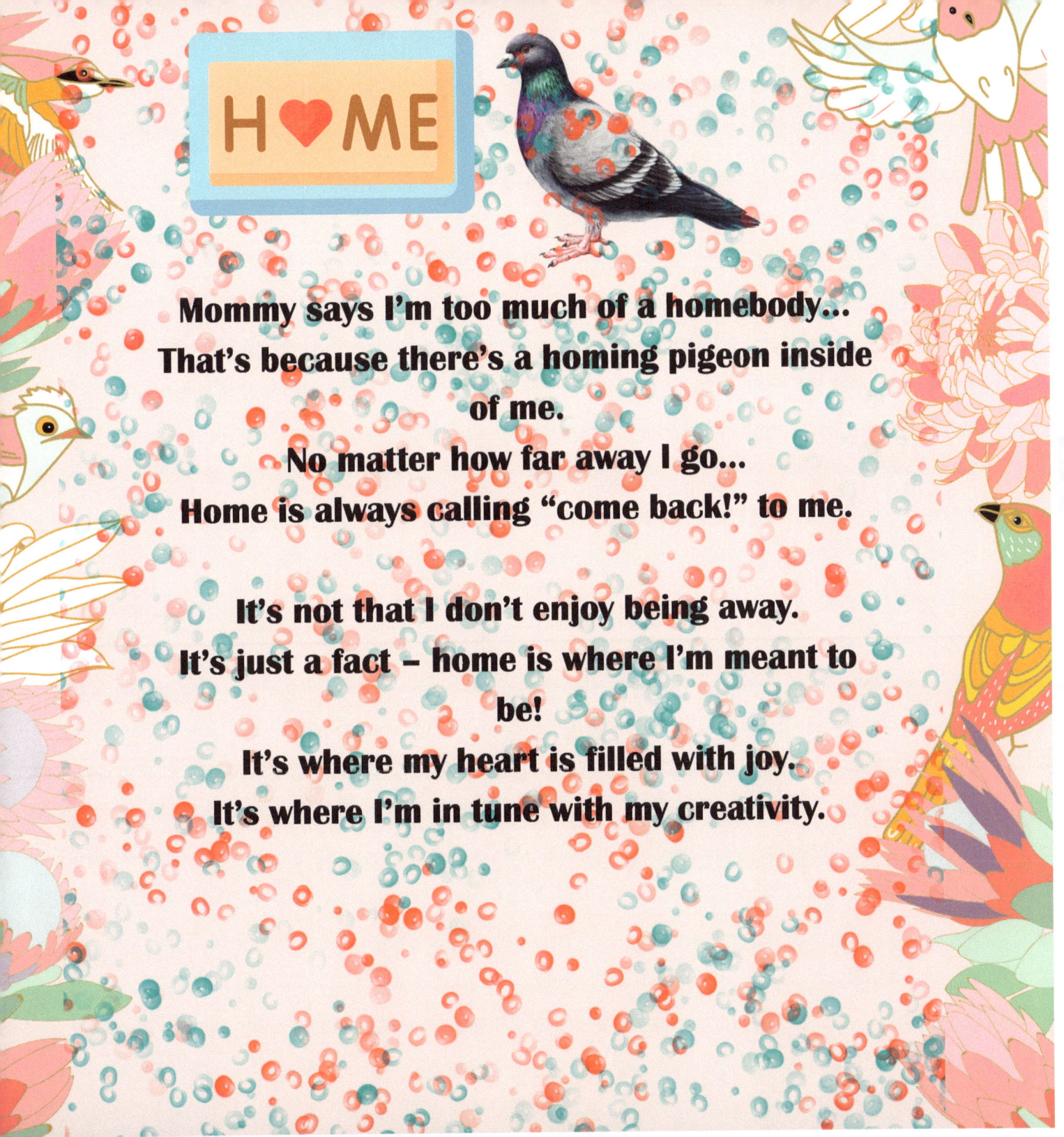

H♥ME

Mommy says I'm too much of a homebody...
That's because there's a homing pigeon inside of me.
No matter how far away I go...
Home is always calling "come back!" to me.

It's not that I don't enjoy being away.
It's just a fact – home is where I'm meant to be!
It's where my heart is filled with joy.
It's where I'm in tune with my creativity.

HOME

My imagination opens its doors...
To every creak in the floor, every knock...
Where my heart beats in tune with... -
My Grandfather's antique clock.

It's where – when my feet need me to dance...
I can dance, giving it all I have to give.
And when I venture outside into the garden...
Where water thoughts pour through me
like a sieve.

Home

So, yes, I guess I am a homebody.
Because there's a homing pigeon inside of me.
A quiet, gentle, fluttering spirit we share...
Home is where we can be the best WE.

MY POEM

MY POEM

ALSO BY CATHY MCGOUGH

POETRY SERIES:

There's a Bookworm Inside of Me! (previous
title There's a Chimpanzee Inside of Me!)

JUMP SERIES:

Jump Like a Caribou!
Jump Like a Kangaroo!
Jump at the Zoo!
Jump and Say P.U.!
Jump and Say Boo!
Jump and Say Valentine's Day Is
For Kids Too!
Jump and Look For a Clue!
Jump and Say Happy Birthday to You!
Jump For Everything Blue!
Jump, Hop and Say Happy Easter To You!
Jump and Say Cock-A-Doodle-Do!
Jump and Sing Da-Do-Do-Do!
Jump and Ask Who? Who?
Jump and Squawk Like a Cockatoo!
Jump and Ask Is It You or Ewe?
Jump and Say There's an Ewww in My Stew!
Jump and Say Merry Christmas To You!
Jump and Cheer Happy New Year!
Jump and Say There's a Moo-Moo in a Tutu!
Jump and Say There's a Hare in My Hair!
Jump and Say My Aunt Ate An Ant!
Jump and Say There's An Aardvark
In The Amusement Park!
Jump and Roar For The Dinosaurs!
Jump and Buzz Like A Bee!
Jump and Flutter Like A Butterfly!
Jump and Pop Like Popcorn!
Jump and Ribbit Like A Frog!
Jump and Snore Like A Koala!

Jump and Snuffle Like A Platypus!
Jump and Grunt Like A Groundhog!
Jump and Say Hello!
Jump and Say Friend!
Jump and Say Peace!
Jump and Say Sky!
Jump and Say Merry Christmas!
Jump and Say Happy New Year!
Jump and Say Fun!
Jump and Say Family!
Jump and Say Jump!

CLAP FOR SERIES:

Clap for 1!
Clap for 2!
Clap for 3!
Clap for 4!
Clap for 5!
Clap for 6!
Clap for 7!
Clap for 8!
Clap for 9!
Clap for 10!

The Cat Who Said Hello
The Three Boulders
Billy Shakespeare
Billie Shakespeare
Learn To Draw With Symmetry
ABC More Learn to Draw With Symmetry

Non-Fiction
103 Fundraising Ideas For Parent Volunteers With Schools and Teams